# Developing children's minds through literacy and numeracy

First published in 1998 by the Institute of Education
University of London, 20 Bedford Way, London WC1H 0AL
Tel: 0171-580 1122. Fax: 0171-612 6126

*Pursuing Excellence in Education*

© Institute of Education University of London 1998

British Library Cataloguing in Publication Data:
a catalogue record for this publication is available
from the British Library

ISBN 0 85473 550 X

---

Typography and design by Joan Rose

Produced in Great Britain by Reprographic Services
Institute of Education University of London

Printed by Formara Limited
16 The Candlemakers, Temple Farm Industrial Estate
Southend on Sea, Essex SS2 5RX


I1-0015-TNIL-0198

INSTITUTE OF EDUCATION
University of London

# Developing children's minds through literacy and numeracy

## Terezinha Nunes

*Professor of Child Development and Learning*

Based on an Inaugural Professorial Lecture
delivered at the
Institute of Education University of London
on 5 February 1998

# Acknowledgements

The Institute of Education, the ESRC, the MRC, the Nuffield Foundation, and the Open University have generously supported the research reported here. My colleagues at the Institute, in particular at the Child Development and Learning and the Mathematical Sciences groups, have created an exciting environment where ideas and research are discussed with enthusiasm. I am very grateful to these people and institutions who have helped me make Britain my new home.

*To Daniel, Julia, and Peter*

Photo by Angela Hobsbaum

*Professor Terezinha Nunes*

# Developing children's minds through literacy and numeracy

Education and psychology have engaged in a challenging and worthwhile exchange on the nature of intelligence and its development in the course of this century. The challenges have resulted in major changes in psychological theories of intelligence and pedagogical approaches to promoting its development. I want to explore in this lecture one psychological perspective on intelligence and its development through schooling, identified as a socio-historical or an activity approach to intelligence. Within this perspective, schools have two extremely important functions in the development of intelligence: to propose to learners new objects for thought and to offer them new tools for thinking with. Both the objects and the tools are socially and historically constructed and change the reasoning activity of subjects as they reason. This way of thinking about intelligence raises provocative questions for education and for psychology. My aim is to consider these questions and some of the hints at what the answers might be. I think we are still a long way from clear answers but the glimpses that we can get now suggest that the exchanges between psychology and education will be even more fascinating in the future.

This paper considers examples of new objects of thought and tools for thinking which are related to the acquisition of literacy and numeracy by weaving together some theoretical issues and results of empirical research. The first section sets out the context for approaching the question of how schools develop children's minds. The following sections deal with literacy and numeracy more specifically.

## Learning facts or encountering new objects of thought?

As we go about in everyday life, we have many exposures to the world but we have no reason to think that the world is round. We see the horizon at the end of a flat ocean or behind the mountains, we see the sky above, and the earth solidly under our feet. In fact, we might have no reason to think about the shape of the world at all, and we do not have any doubts about what 'up' and 'down' mean. One day in school, perhaps when we are five or six years old, the teacher tells us that the world is round. It might seem that all we are learning is a 'fact' – and perhaps one rather irrelevant to our lives for that matter. These days the teacher might even show a picture of the world taken from a satellite: the world is round and we can see it. But research on how children deal with this fact suggests that this information can be much more than a fact: it can become a new object of thought and a framework for thinking about the world.

The evidence for the need to distinguish between learning a fact and encountering a new object of thought is simple: children might learn the fact but not understand the thinking framework that goes with it. Researchers like Nussbaum and Novack (Nussbaum, 1985; Nussbaum and Novack, 1976; also Vosniadou and Brewer, 1992) have documented this by asking children a series of questions to be answered through drawings and words. My interviews with Lucas and Frances (Nunes, 1995) follow in general format the interview designed by Nussbaum and colleagues.

Lucas (6 years) and Frances (8 years) were asked to imagine that they were astronauts and to draw the world as they would see it from their spaceship. They were then asked to draw some countries, some people, clouds and rain. Both children knew that the world is round and drew it round. Lucas put great care into drawing the countries (Figure 1)[1]. His outlines of South America and England are quite good. He also drew in Australia, which he thought was not well accomplished but which was clearly placed in the Southern hemisphere, and then he threw in a couple more countries. Frances was much less keen to identify the countries and obtain the correct shapes but did draw in a North Pole and a South Pole. Their drawings do not differ very much up to this point. However, when we look at the people in the countries, the clouds, and the rain, we notice a considerable difference. Lucas uses a flat world conception: the people all have the same orientation as do the clouds and the rainfall. He drew a round world and used a flat conception, with one 'up' and one 'down' .

*Figure 1: Two pictures of the earth*

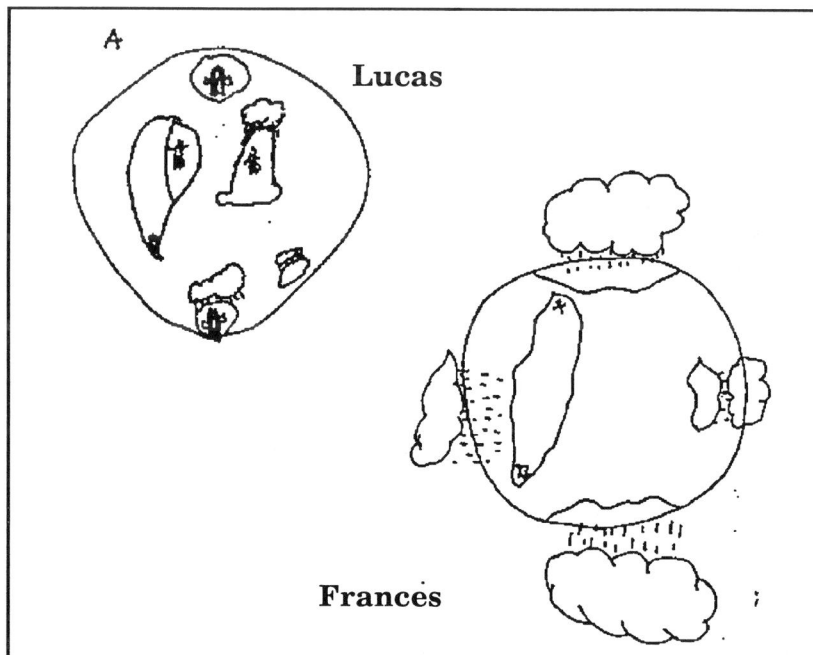

Frances, in contrast, has the clouds above placed all around the world, and the rain falling from the clouds down to the earth in four different directions. This is a different way of thinking about 'up' and 'down': 'up' is away from the centre and 'down' is towards the centre of the world.

Lucas and Frances can go about their lives and talk to each other without the slightest suspicion that they do not think alike. But school has changed Frances's thinking and accomplished something remarkable. It created for her an object of thought and a way of thinking about the world within just a few years, a way of thinking that historically took centuries to develop and the genius of Pythagoras to demonstrate.

Although himself not a proponent of the socio-historical view of intelligence, Piaget (1995/1965) made this point in a forceful way. Following Koyré (1898), he suggested that it is possible to speak of veritable intellectual mutations of the human intellect in the course of history, which are later transmitted as ways of thinking in the culture and offer young people new hypotheses for understanding the world. These transformations of thought allow ideas which have been 'painfully invented by the greatest geniuses to become, not merely accessible, but even easy and obvious to schoolchildren' (p. 37). This does not suggest that children's minds are passive, as Piaget emphasizes, but rather that schools furnish 'the elements and the model for a possible construction'.

Adolescents do not start studying genetics today from the same point that Mendel did. Rather than starting from observations, students start from a different object of thought, the concept of gene, a symbolic object historically constructed. Like the conception of a round world, the idea of genes being involved in the transmission of information across generations altered our basic ways of thinking about heredity and hereditary traits. Although genes were theoretical entities for Mendel, we can now treat them as 'things'. For students' intellectual development, though, what matters is to encounter genes as objects of thought. The vocabulary and some facts about genes have become part of the wider society outside schools and research laboratories but it is likely that this is another case of a round world: the way of thinking that goes with the facts about genes is accomplished when genes become an object of thought, most likely at school and in research laboratories.

It is quite possible that not all the facts that we learn in school are the same sort of symbolic object as the round world and genes. They are not all intellectual mutations. If we simply learn that two plus two is four, an 'addition fact', this might have little impact on our way of thinking. It is equally possible that real intellectual mutations might be learned in school without consequences for how the learner thinks: the fact is learned but not the framework that goes with it. These dead-ends in no way confront the thesis that schools can offer students new objects for thought which can change the students' thinking frameworks in profound ways. The question is not whether some things are facts to be learned and others are theories, hypotheses, or ways of thinking. Much of what schools can do for children's intellectual development may depend on whether the learned facts have been taught as 'mere acquisitions' or whether they have become objects of thought and tools for thinking with.

## Reading and writing as new activities

Literacy can be taught as a mere acquisition, and this is all that Piaget (1995), for example, believed that literacy is. Literacy as a mere acquisition rests on the Aristotelian assumption that writing is the transcription of speech (Olson, 1996). In this view, what children learn when they learn an alphabetic script is which letters to use in order to write down which sounds. Reading is the other side of the coin: knowing which sounds to produce when the letters are recognized. This Aristotelian view can be shown to be at fault when it is analyzed from the perspective of activity theory. Literacy *as an activity* differs from speaking and creates both a new object of thought and a new tool for thinking. This is why literacy can develop children's minds.

Literacy differs from oral communication in many ways. The first difference is pragmatic. A fascinating example is offered by Ferreiro (1992). Ana, a 6 year old girl who lives in Mexico, receives a letter from her grandmother, who lives in Argentina. Ana has learned to read and write and decides to reply immediately. She is used to receiving letters and knows the rituals of opening. She writes: 'Dear Grandmother'. Then she asks her mother to read the letter because she can't read the grandmother's handwriting. As the mother reads, she writes her reply. The mother reads: 'This letter will arrive on your birthday and I want to wish you a happy birthday'. Ana writes: 'Thank you'. The mother reads: 'I am looking forward to your coming and spend hours planning what we are going to do and the lovely places we will visit together when you come'. Ana writes: 'I knew you would'. The mother reads a passage where the grandmother asks about the new house they are going to buy. Ana decides this is not meant for her to answer and writes: 'Mummy will write to you'. The mother reads: 'Thank you for the beautiful ashtray you sent me. I really loved it'. Ana writes: 'That's why we sent it.' The mother reads a passage where the grandmother asks how are her brother and sister and Ana writes: 'Fine'. The mother reads the final greetings and Ana writes a request to the grandmother: 'OK, I would like you to write in block letters. Thank you for sending us a letter. Signature Ana granddaughter' (p 97-99)[2].

Ana's final text reads: 'Dear grandmother. Thank you. I knew you would. Mummy will write to you. That's why we sent it. Fine. OK, I would like you to write in block letters. Thank you for sending us a letter. Signature Ana granddaughter'.

Ana's reply to her grandmother's letter is an illustration of some changes in language use that result from writing: question-answer interactions, easily mastered by children in oral, face-to-face communication, have to be transformed radically if communication is to be accomplished through letters. The old function, question-answer interaction, in the new form of language, written, is transformed into a new activity. Literacy enables and constrains communication in ways that are related to the tool being used. Communication is enabled because Ana can communicate with her grandmother in spite of distance and time; the constraint is that direct answers do not communicate, the question must be in some way restored as the answer is provided.

The story of Ana's letter does not end there. Ana's mother did not mail the letter immediately and Ana found it at a later date. When she read her own letter without having the Grandmother's letter at the same time, she realized that the letter could not be understood and set out to improve on its communicative effectiveness. She made her own message into an object of thought and considerably improved it.

Literacy does not simply change the activity of communicating: it also creates new objects of thought, a script and a text. What are the consequences of thinking about these new symbolic objects?

## a. Scripts as objects of thought

A script is a *system for the representation of language.* To be competent users of a script, learners need to understand how the language is represented. Languages can be represented in many ways. A script may have one sign for each syllable; this is what is called a syllabic script. Or it may have one sign for each phoneme, and be an instance of an alphabetic script. English is a morpho-phonic script (Venezky, 1995): letters are used to represent sounds and morphemes. Often there is no conflict between representing sounds and morphemes but sometimes there is a conflict, and the representation of morphemes comes through the holes in the letter-sound relations. A simple example to begin with: the phonemes /t/ and /d/ are often represented by the letters 't' and 'd' but when these sounds are at the end of past regular verbs we use a fixed spelling for both of these sounds, 'ed'. We say /kist/ but spell 'kissed' and say /kild/ but spell 'killed'. How do children come to understand this complex way of representing oral English? What do they gain by understanding this new object of thought, the script?

Much research had already been done on the phonic side of English spelling and other languages. This research tells the story of an intriguing interaction between children's minds and scripts as objects of thought. In order to understand how scripts work, children must become aware of the sounds of words, which is by no means a simple task. Bryant and Bradley (1985) showed this in a study that combined the strengths of longitudinal and experimental investigations. The longitudinal investigation showed that children's progress in reading and writing was strongly related to and predicted by their awareness of the sounds in words before they could read any words. The greater the children's awareness of sounds before learning to read, the better they learned to read and write when they were in school. This correlation remained significant over a four year period and even after controlling for the effects that general verbal ability might have on the relation between awareness of sounds and learning to read. This control is extremely important because the correlation between awareness of sounds and learning to read could have resulted only from the fact that both are related to general verbal ability. Without the control, we would not know whether there is a specific relation between awareness of sounds and literacy learning.

Bryant and Bradley's results have been replicated in a number of studies and with different languages that use alphabetic representation (see, for example, Lundberg, Frost, and Petersen, 1988). This replicability is very important in science and gives researchers confidence in the results. They also observed more than this predictive relation: they showed that there is a mutual enhancing between awareness of sounds and literacy learning. They did so by teaching two groups of children to classify words by their sounds. One of the groups simply practised the sound categorization and did not use letters in their exercises. The second group of children practised this categorization by putting together words like 'car' and 'cup', because they both start with the same sound, and also identified the letter which the words had in common, as they were helped to spell these words with moveable plastic letters. The children who had practised sound categorization made more progress in literacy than a control group of children, who practised another type of word categorization instead, but the difference was only significant for the group who practised sound categorization and had the letters to represent the sounds. Having the letters may help the children anchor the sound similarity: they now have a label for the class, 'words that start with c' (Carraher, 1987). Olson suggests that this mutual enhancing between awareness of sounds and learning an alphabetic script goes even further: 'the script provides the model for thinking about the sound structure of speech' (1996:147).

Olson goes on to suggest that 'knowledge of phonology may have little impact on thinking' (p.147), and in a sense dismisses this insight into scripts as of little consequence. However, research does not support his dismissive attitude. Learning a script is like learning that the world is round: it is learning a framework for thinking about language and writing. When we learn to read a second language, we already have a framework for learning scripts and benefit from it.

There are three types of evidence for this. The first type of evidence was provided by Scribner and Cole (1981) in their analysis of the consequences of literacy amongst the Vai people in Liberia. They compared literate and non-literate adults in a task that involved learning a novel script, a rebus, where the names of objects in pictures were used as phonological elements to represent new meanings, as illustrated in Figure 2 (adapted

*Figure 2: A rebus sentence*

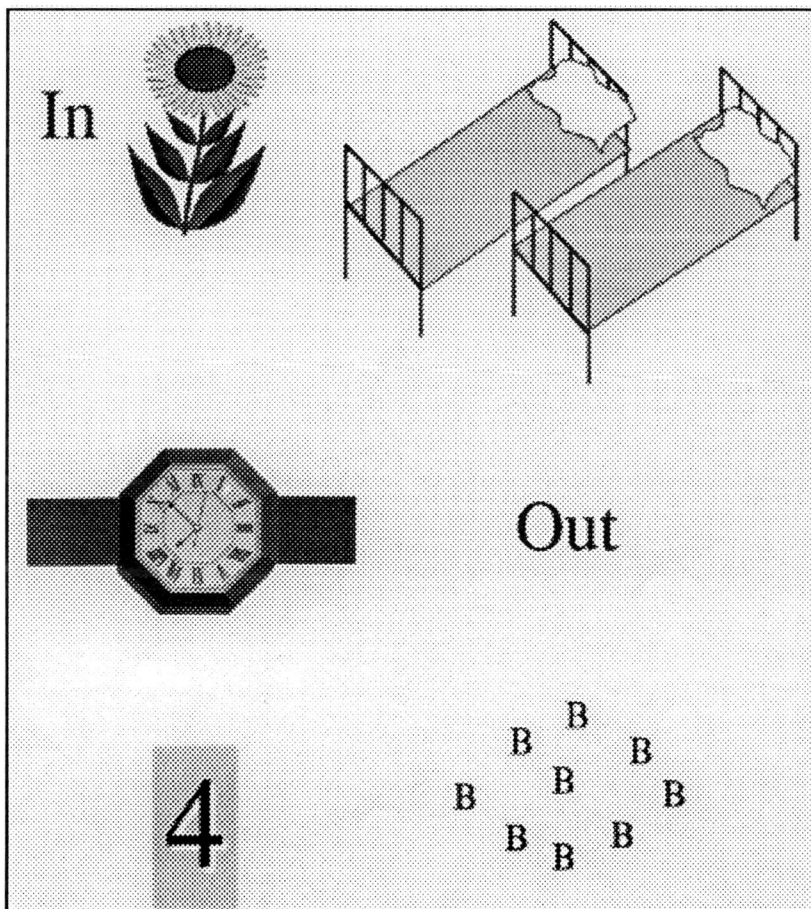

from Scribner and Cole, 1981). Their aim in using a novel script was to investigate whether the literate adults would learn it more easily than the non-literate adults. If the literate adults have actually acquired a framework for thinking about scripts, they should clearly learn a new script more easily than the adults who had not yet acquired this framework. The literate adults had learned to read either a syllabic script, Vai (used for everyday purposes), or an alphabetic script, either Arabic (used in religious contexts) or English (used in school). Although the scripts differed in the unit of sound represented by the graphic signs, all three used phonological representation. The literate adults did in fact learn the new script more easily than the non-literates and were also more ingenious in using pictures to write with. They had acquired a way of thinking about scripts which simplified their learning.

The other two lines of evidence come from work on bilingual, biliterate children. Children learning to read two alphabetic scripts probably develop a single framework for thinking about scripts, which they use across languages. If this is the case, two things follow. First, the children's ability to analyse the sounds of language, to read and to spell should be intercorrelated across their two languages even after partialling out the effects that their general verbal ability might have on this relation. There is in fact much evidence supporting this prediction from a variety of studies with bilingual, biliterate children. Included are studies with Arabic and French biliterates (Wagner, Spratt and Ezzaki, 1989), Portuguese and English (da Fontoura and Siegel, 1991) and Hebrew and English (Geva, Wade-Woolley and Shany, 1993). Some of this evidence was obtained by my colleagues Anna Gowing (1994) and Miriam Bindman (1997) while they were working at the Institute of Education towards their degrees. The evidence is particularly strong in the studies where the children are learning two alphabetic scripts that use different letters, like English and Hebrew. They cannot use specific knowledge of letter values – such as 'b' represents the sound /b/ – across scripts: they can only use the same framework for thinking about scripts. The second prediction that can be made about biliterate children is that they will become better learners of scripts than monoliterate children of the same general verbal ability. When a framework for thinking about scripts can be used across two languages, the learner has the opportunity of applying the same model to two objects and should have greater insight into the model itself. Research comparing children learning to read and write a second language with monolingual children of the same general level of verbal ability does in fact show that biliterate children read and spell significantly better than the monolingual children in the one language which they have in common. Bindman's (1997) results are particularly impressive here because the biliterate children in her study were learning to use different letters across scripts. Bindman concludes that the knowledge that the children can use across languages must be of an abstract nature – a framework for thinking about language – rather than the specific knowledge of the sounds of each language and the letters that represent these sounds.

Together these three types of results offer clear evidence that learning about the representation of sounds through written signs is not without consequences for thinking: once the framework is acquired in one language, it can be used when we learn to read a second language.

Much less is known about the other aspect of written English, the morphemic side of the script, and whether it can also become a framework for thinking about language. In the last few years, Peter Bryant, Miriam Bindman and I carried out a series of studies to examine how the morphological aspect of the English script is mastered and its consequences for thinking about language. We expected that the story of its acquisition would be in some ways quite similar to that of the phonic side: we expected a mutual enhancing between children's initial awareness of morphemes and literacy learning.

We carried out a three-year longitudinal study and assessed the children's awareness of morphology several times during this period. This assessment was obtained through the children's ability to make morphological analogies at the level of word transformations (e.g., 'teacher' is to 'taught' as 'writer' is to what?) or sentence transformations (for a full description of these measures, see Nunes, Bryant, and Bindman, 1997). We also assessed their use of spellings that reflect morphology in a variety of ways.

One measure of morphological spelling considered whether the children used 'ed' at the end of past regular verbs for the /t/ and /d/ sounds but not at the end of other words. As can be seen from the spellings in Figure 3, the correct use of 'ed' cannot be taken for granted.

**Figure 3:** *Three children's spellings for some of the words used by Nunes, Bryant, and Bindman (1997)*

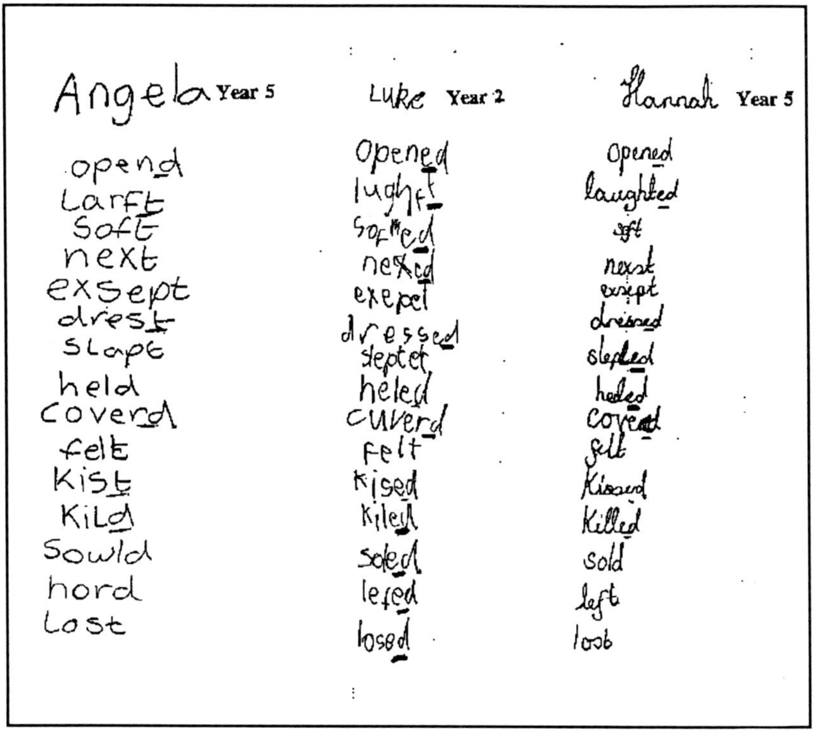

A second measure considered whether the children used the 'wh' spelling for interrogatives, although the 'h' does not make any contribution to the reading of words like 'when' and 'what' in the local UK pronunciation (the study was conducted in London and Oxford) and the 'w' makes no contribution to the reading of 'who'. Figure 4 shows that the use of 'wh' is not a simple matter either, even though the number of interrogative words is so reduced that it could in principle simply be memorized.

A third measure looked at whether the children spelled consistently words which share a stem in spite of a change in the phonology across the words. Some examples are offered in Figure 5

**Figure 4:** *The spelling of interrogatives by three children*

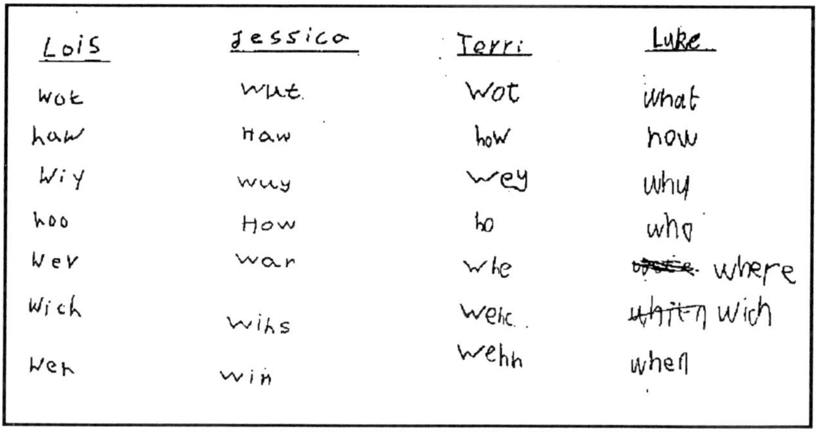

| Lois | Jessica | Terri | Luke |
|------|---------|-------|------|
| wok | wut | wot | what |
| haw | naw | how | how |
| Wiy | wuy | wey | why |
| hoo | How | ho | who |
| Wev | war | whe | ~~wse~~ where |
| Wich | wihs | wehc | ~~whien~~ wich |
| Weh | win | wehh | when |

**Figure 5:** *The spelling of words with the same stem*

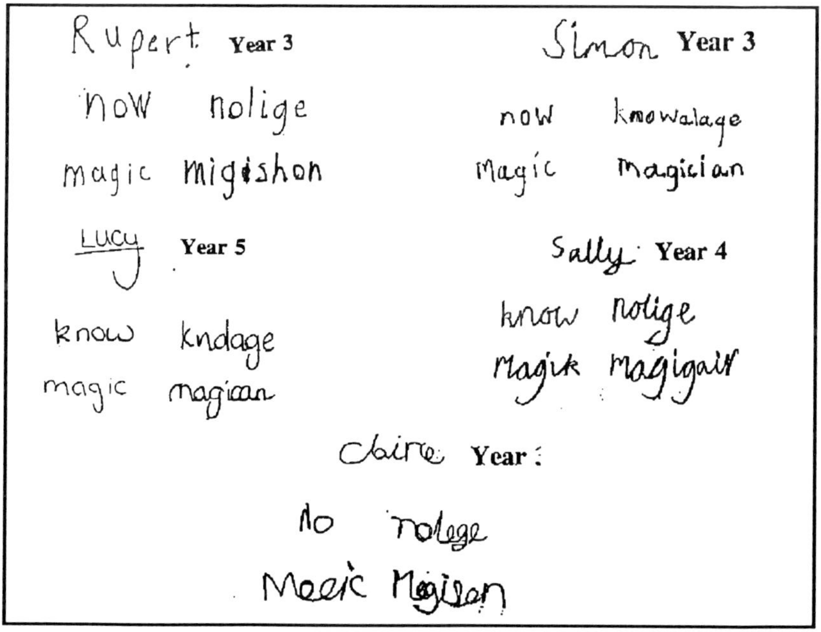

Rupert **Year 3**
now  nolige
magic  migishon

Simon **Year 3**
now  knowalage
magic  magician

Lucy **Year 5**
know  kndage
magic  magican

Sally **Year 4**
know  nolige
magik  magigall

Claire **Year ?**
no  nolege
Magic  Magian

The fourth measure looked at consistency in the use of a stem when one of the stimuli was actually a pseudo-word – that is, a sequence of sounds that used a real stem and a real suffix in a non-existing combination in the English language. The pseudo-words in this task were dinosaur names, made of a stem, like 'knot', and a suffix, 'saurus'. The stems chosen for the dinosaur names included silent letters (the 'k' in knot; the 'r' in 'iron', which is not pronounced in the local English dialect) or digraphs; these spelling difficulties ensured that, when the children knew how to spell the stem and reproduced this spelling in the dinosaur name, they were not simply spelling the pseudo-word phonetically. Pictures of the knotosaurus and the ironsaurus are included in Figure 6 to show why we expected the children to use the consistent spelling for the stem. To test the children's consistency in the spelling of stems, we saw the children on two different days; they spelled one word on one day and the second word on a different day. This meant that they could not copy one spelling from the other.

The first question that we examined concerned the acquisition of the morphological aspect of written English. This acquisition showed an overall pattern quite similar to that of phonological aspects. Children's awareness of morphology was significantly related to their adoption of morphological spelling strategies even when the spelling was assessed two years after the morphological awareness and after partialling out the effects of their general verbal ability. This was the case irrespective of which one of the four measures of morphological spelling was considered. But children's spelling of morphemes at an earlier age also predicted their awareness of morphology at a later age. In fact, the best way to predict children's adoption of morphological spellings at a later age was to write an equation which used as predictors their awareness of morphology, their spelling, and a factor for the interaction between these two measures. These findings suggest that children's awareness of morphology and their learning of morphological spellings enhance each other in the same way that phonological awareness and learning letters do.

The second question we examined was whether learning about morphological spellings was like learning that the world is round. Does this learning provide a framework for thinking about language or is this a case of a mere acquisition with no consequences for thinking? If children

***Figure 6:*** *The knotosaurus, the ironsaurus and some spellings of their names*

Rupert
**Year 3**

note
hoter-soros

Amy
**Year 5**

Knot
Knotasoreaus.

Charmaine
**Year 4**

Knot
Knotersaurus

Rupert **Year 3**
Iern
I ern ar— soros

Charmaine **Year 4**

iron
Ironasaurus

Pierre **Year 5**

lyon
ianasawrus

Georgena **Year 5**

Iron
Iunasauras

learn a morphological framework for thinking about language, they should become better at interpreting novel words when these can be analyzed into morphological components. This would be a very useful framework indeed: when faced with a completely new word, perhaps in a science text, the children would not necessarily flounder. If they know the morphemes as elements of meaning from other words, they might have a good shot at interpreting the novel one. For example, a child with a morphological framework for thinking about language may realize that 'bicycle' is a vehicle with two wheels and 'tricycle' is one with three wheels and connect 'bi-' with the meaning 'two of something'. When first encountered, words like 'binocular', 'bipedal' and 'bidirectional' may appear less unfamiliar to this child than to another with less morphological insight.

We investigated the possibility that the acquisition of morphological spellings provides children with a framework for thinking about language by testing whether the children's use of morphological spellings was significantly related to their ability to interpret novel words. To make sure that the words were really novel and had not been encountered before, we created the words ourselves by joining a real stem and a real affix in a new combination. These pseudo-words were presented to the children either in sentences (for example: 'He wants to *unclimb* the hill as quickly as possible') or on their own (unclimb). The children were asked to say what they thought that word meant. For each interpretation the children were given one point if they had used information from both the stem and the affix in order to produce the definition. We used the four measures of morphological spellings described earlier on as predictors of the children's ability to interpret novel words. The correlation between the spelling tasks and the children's success in interpreting novel words, which was tested either six or eight months after the spelling, was significant for all four measures and remained significant for the first three even after we partialled out the effects of general verbal ability (the last measure just missed significance). These results support the idea that children do learn a framework for thinking about language when they master morphological spellings.

## b. *Texts as objects of and tools for thought*

A number of researchers (Goody and Watt, 1963; Luria, 1976; Olson, 1976) have suggested that the possibility of analyzing the form of a message by writing it down has considerable impact on the development of logic. Although plausible, this hypothesis has so far eluded adequate testing possibly because it is a hypothesis with many parts and angles to it.

First, how do we know that a literate person has in fact taken texts as objects of thought? Although the ability to read and write per se should be sufficient evidence that scripts have become objects of thought, things may be different as far as taking texts as object of thought. The case of Ana's letter to her Grandmother illustrates that thinking about texts is not the same activity as using a script to read and write. In her first attempt, Ana wrote to her Grandmother without thinking about the text itself. It may be necessary to ensure that literacy learners are engaged in the activity of thinking about text to obtain effects on logical reasoning.

Second, there may be many links between thinking about texts and logical reasoning. Perhaps only a coordinated investigation considering these different links can offer a good test of the hypothesis. Olson and his colleagues, for example (Robinson, Goelman, and Olson, 1983; Torrance, Lee, and Olson, 1992; Olson, 1996), have suggested that the distinction between what is said and what is meant is essential for understanding syllogistic reasoning and that becoming literate makes this distinction more accessible to children. They showed that older, literate children were better at making the distinction than younger, preliterate children. However, literacy learning, age and level of verbal ability were confounded in these studies and we cannot come to any conclusions regarding the impact of literacy on children's ability to distinguish what is said from what is meant. But even without such confounding, this research is still a long way from showing that children's logical reasoning changes when they become literate because the link between distinguishing what is said from what is meant and syllogistic reasoning was not investigated.

It is also possible that the hypothesis is taking the wrong angle: the main effect of literacy on reasoning may not be a consequence of having writing as an object of thought but rather as an instrument of thought. Perhaps we don't learn new frameworks for reasoning from thinking about text but are just more proficient in carrying out our reasoning – just as we are more proficient when we solve sums involving large numbers using a calculator rather than pencil and paper. As I write this text, I can go over it many times. Unlike conversation, I can read later on what I have written before and decide that I have not written what I had in mind. I can change the writing and leave no trace from the earlier drafts. What had come at the end, rather like a conclusion, may on second thoughts be more like a premise, and might be moved to the beginning. The same function – to achieve a thought-through argument – can be accomplished in two different ways, in oral or in written form, but the activity of producing the argument may be itself rather different. Thinking about text or about oral language are different activities even if the framework that we use for thinking is the same.

If the impact of writing on reasoning is through its use as a tool for thinking, not as an object of thought, then we have been designing the wrong studies. The research that we need should be about within-individual differences and should show that the same people perform reasoning tasks differently when they have different tools for thinking, oral or written language. We could then ask what changes and what remains the same when we use these different tools.

One obvious change, which was emphasized by Goody (1987), was not in reasoning per se but in the literate person's range of action. Goody studied, amongst others, the records by Ansumana Sonie in Vai script in 1926, when Sonie was acting as middleman for a variety of transactions, customers, and items in a way that differed significantly from the pre-literate trading activity more frequent at the time, which tended to concentrate upon a single item or a limited range of goods with relatively fixed prices. Goody comments:

> A limited amount of the kind of information Sonie recorded here can be held in memory store. But it cannot be subjected to the same kind of checking and addition that is possible when it is preserved in graphic form. In particular, it is difficult to see how he could otherwise keep track simultaneously of sales by type of goods and by date of sale. These bookkeeping operations,

however, were critical to the expansion of Sonie's commercial activities. They enabled him to deal with a wider range of goods and to make a finer calculation of profit and loss (1987:197).

With literacy, memory was not a limit for Sonie's business, in contrast to what happened to those men engaged in commerce who had to rely on memory. His range of action was drastically influenced by literacy. This uncomplicated example illustrates rather well how writing as a tool changes our activities: we can circumvent our biological limitations as long as we use the tool. Literates do not need a better memory than non-literates because they are not bound by their natural mnemonic limits. Activity theory differs from traditional theories of intellectual development exactly because it takes the activity, not the individual, as the unit of analysis. When the individual is engaged in an activity with a tool, it is the system composed by the individual with the tool that is considered. To draw the limits of the individual at the boundary of the skin makes the activity incomprehensible (see Bateson, 1972, for a fascinating example). But this is exactly what research comparing literates and non-literates all working in the oral mode has done: the literates were separated from their tool and, in these circumstances, they were not very different from the non-literates, including in their memory ability (Scribner and Cole, 1981).

Another obvious change that comes with literacy is in the breadth of possible contacts and exposure to others' thinking. Ana, living in Mexico, was in contact with her Grandmother who lived in Argentina. We can read the works of many people, living or dead, whom we will never meet, and can be inspired by them. This is an easy but deeply felt truth amongst academics, I suspect. Outside school, literates can also use networks and sources that they could not use without writing. Hamilton (1997), for example, has shown through careful ethnographic work how people can expand their knowledge through their own investment in activities that involve literacy. The activities which she documented – such as finding out more about one's medical condition or becoming a dedicated fan – were not those which schools normally recognize or value as literate. Perhaps these were mere acquisitions and did not create frameworks for thinking but perhaps they did. Literacy practices lead to the development of vernacular knowledge, Hamilton suggests. In this process of investigation of others' ideas, we may come across someone that suggests that the world is round. Literacy as a tool probably does not work according to a simple cause and effect model but rather as the source of new possibilities, which may or may not be taken up.

## The enabling tools of numeracy

There are so many activities in our lives that we cannot carry out without using numbers that it is easy for numbers to go unnoticed. The teacher is asked in the morning: are all your students here today? She can quickly do a head count and answer the question. She might not have been able to tell without counting. The nurse measures out the amount of medicine with a 5 ml spoon. Estimation might not be a good idea here. The girl measures the dog's bed and goes to the shop to buy a mattress. Her memory for sizes just would not be good enough to choose the right mattress. When activities will go wrong if we are not precise about quantities, we often use measurement and number to go beyond our perceptual and mnemonic limits. We are hardly aware of our natural limitations when we use the numeracy tools which have been developed over the course of history by cultural groups.

The very activity of counting would be beyond the constraints of human memory without the support of culturally invented systems. As pointed out by Gelman and Gallistel (1978), counting requires that we respect three principles. In order to be able to count properly, we need to:

1.   have a different counting label for each object;
2.   set the counting labels and the objects in one-to-one correspondence; and
3.   use the counting labels in a fixed order.

The first two requirements are relatively easy to meet but the last one can be rather difficult when we consider the limits of human memory: to remember, for example, 1,000 words in a fixed order is not an easy task.

Over the course of history, cultures have developed counting systems which help us cope with this requirement. Instead of having completely different words as we have, say for fruits and flowers, we use recursiveness: we learn a small set of labels in a fixed order and also ways of using them in new combinations over and over again, always in the same order, to generate new number labels. We don't in fact need to *learn* the thousand words: we can generate them in the correct order even if we never heard them all in sequence. However marvellous this cultural accomplishment is for its power to help us overcome natural memory limits, this is not all that there is to numbers. Once we learn numbers and other mathematical systems of signs, they can become objects of thought and tools to think with. This is only the beginning.

## a. Numbers as object of thought

Numeracy, like literacy, can be viewed as a mere acquisition without consequences for the mind. In this view, learning number would be like learning tokens to tag old ideas about numerosity with. The parallel to the Aristotelian view of literacy in number learning is very much alive today in psychological research about infants' understanding of numerosity and the acquisition of the counting string. Although it is important to know about these studies, they contribute little to our understanding of numbers as frameworks for thinking because they do not capture the core issues in numeracy. In the same way that literacy is not mostly about knowing that the letter 'b' represents the sound /b/ and not the sound /t/ (even though this bit of knowledge is included in literacy), the power of numeracy is not a matter of knowing that a display with two objects is different from a display with three objects (which can be done without counting, incidentally) or that 'two plus two equals four' (which can be done without understanding number).

However lamentable it may seem, teaching can be carried out as if counting, writing numbers and learning basic facts and algorithms are the essence of numeracy. But numbers do offer and can be learned as frameworks for thinking. Mathematics is, above all other things, a source of models for thinking.

Numbers are symbols within systems of representation, which offer models for thinking about the world. A significant advantage of models is that we can find out about the world by manipulating the model in a way that we might not be able to operate on the world. For example, if we want to build something which will be exposed to heat and make sure that it does not explode, we can calculate the parameters that describe under what condition our object would explode – and then avoid the explosion altogether. As long as we are operating on a model that describes well the relations in the situation, we can be confident that we can prevent the explosion. But in order to know whether our predictions make any sense, we need to think about what the numbers mean or how they model the situation. An example contrasting numbers with different meanings and within different systems can clarify this point.

The example is simple: it is about joining two quantities. Figure 7 shows two glasses of milk. One glass contains 80 dl and the other 20 dl. When we pour the milk from the two glasses into the larger container next to them, we can predict the level that the milk will reach in the container. We know the level the milk will reach before we pour because we can operate on the numbers. The ability to predict is one advantage of models.

Figure 8 shows two glasses of orange juice. One glass contains juice which is made with 80 per cent orange concentrate; the other contains juice made with 20 per cent orange concentrate. What will the concentration of orange juice be when we pour the juice from the two glasses into the large jar?

Why don't we obtain the same result in the two examples? Although the numbers are the same, they are numbers within different systems. In the first example, the numbers are used as models of extensive quantities, which are measured through the successive application of a unit of the same nature until the total is accounted for. If we were to take one decilitre at a time from the first glass, after 40 such operations, there would be 40 dl left. In extensive quantities, the total is equal to the sum of the parts. The number in this measurement operation indicates how many parts in the whole. In the second example, the numbers are used to represent a ratio between two quantities, orange concentrate and water. The expression 80 per cent concentrate leaves implicit the fact that 20 per cent of the juice is made of

*Figure 7: How much milk when we join the milk from two containers*

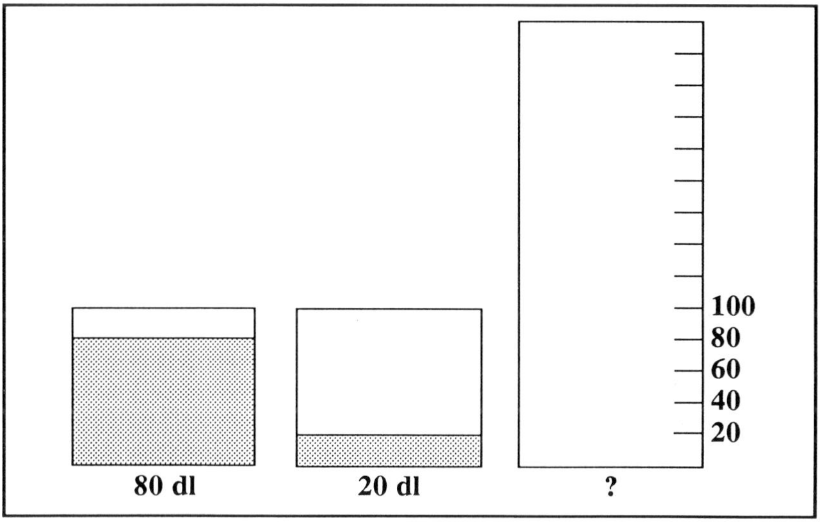

80 dl    20 dl    ?

*Figure 8: What is the concentration of the juice when we join the juice in the two containers?*

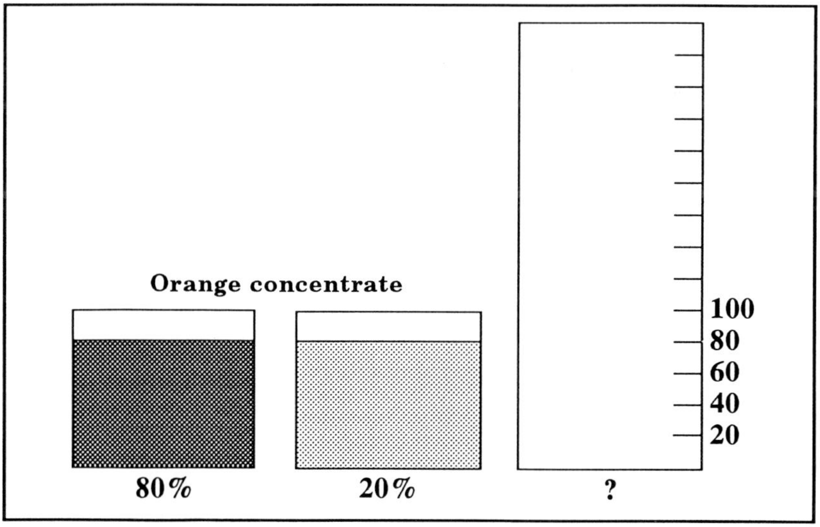

Orange concentrate

80%    20%    ?

water. The number in this measure is a ratio. Taking juice away from the glass does not alter its concentration (as long as it is uniformly mixed): amount of juice and ratio between orange concentrate and water are independent of each other. The part-whole relation between the measured object and the unit, on one hand, and a ratio between two variables, on the other hand, can be represented using the same numerical tokens but their meaning within the system is rather different. The numbers in Figures 7 and 8 are part of two different frameworks for thinking about quantities.

The difference between these two types of number was described by Freudenthal (1983) as phenomenologically related to the expression 'relatively', which may remain implicit or be explicitly verbalized, and which applies to the second type of number, to intensive quantities. Freudenthal suggests that this 'relatively' gives meaning to sentences such as 'A flea can jump higher than a man' or to statements such as 'This tea is sweeter' when the same amount of sugar was put into two cups of tea but one cup has double the tea in it. Whereas extensive quantities can be compared directly – how much sugar is put in each cup – intensive quantities must be normed or scaled before they are compared – to make the tea in the two cups just as sweet, you use half the amount of sugar for the cup that contains half the amount of tea.

Research shows that schools cannot take for granted that children understand the difference between these two types of number. Despina Desli, working here at the Institute, asked students in primary school to predict the results of joining or sampling from intensive quantities (Desli and Nunes, 1997). Among her examples were the saturatedness of red paint and the taste of orange juice. The children were asked to predict, for example, how saturated the mixture of two tones of red paint would be by identifying the resulting tone in a scale that varied from no red (that is, a white patch) to highly saturated red. The majority of the younger children (7 and 8 year olds) did not choose the same tone of red when two containers with paint of the same red were to be joined: their preferred response in this case was a darker tone. Asking children about the results of sampling from a container with orange juice yielded comparable results: the majority of the younger children expected the sample to be less orangey than the juice in the large jar. A small percentage of 10 year olds still appeared to treat operations with intensive quantities as if they were extensive. Her results confirmed previous findings on children's difficulties with intensive quantities (e.g., Piaget and Inhelder, 1975; Karplus, Pulos, and Stage, 1983; Erickson, 1985) even though she simplified the task by using a visual display for the children's answers and by working with more ordinary quantities than some of those investigated before (e.g., Piaget and Inhelder investigated probability; Erickson investigated temperature).

This example illustrates why numbers cannot be treated as straight-forward representation of numerosity: they acquire meaning as part of a system that models relations between quantities. Numeracy creates new objects of thought when we examine what the numbers mean, what sort of quantity they represent. Quantities can be classified with respect to their properties. Freudenthal (1983) suggests that we can become more aware of the differences between types of quantities by thinking what the numbers in a comparison mean or what numerical operations model actions on the quantities. Does it make sense to make direct comparisons between quantities or do we need to norm the comparison? When we double the quantity, does the value double also? Different types of quantities are modelled through different systems of representation. Amazingly, the same tokens (oral numbers, written numbers) are used across systems with different meanings.

Many mathematical tools create new objects for thought. Think of the case of graphs. If we were to systematically combine shapes and colours to design all the possible coloured shapes, we could then draw a graph where we represent the number of coloured figures as a function of the number of shapes and the number of colours used (see Figure 9). For each number of colours, we will draw a different line. When we finish drawing the graph, we can look at the results and say 'this is a linear function'. The adjective 'linear' applies to the drawing; the function is an object of thought that we created and made visible through drawing the graph. We can then speak about families of functions, such as linear functions, exponential functions etc., and describe each family by an expression about the quantitative relations between the variables.

Data bases constitute another numeracy tool which can create objects of thought for children. Imagine that a student wants to answer the question:

*Figure 9: Number of coloured shapes as a function of the number of shapes and the number of colours*

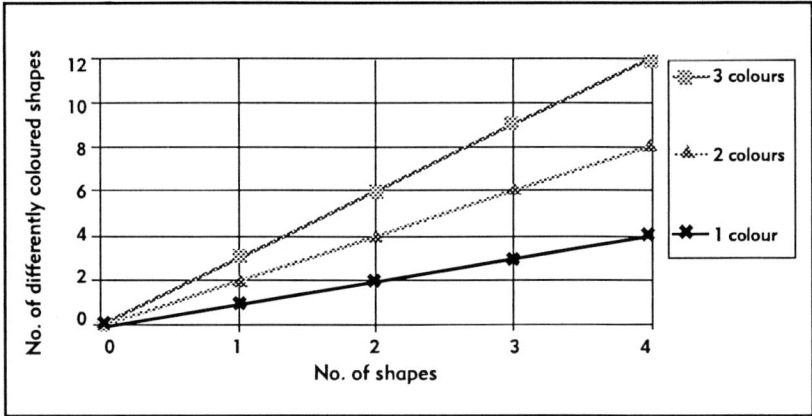

Are girls better than boys at French? She is using a computer data base and needs to put in the grades for each student in the school. She writes into the data base a list of children and a list of grades and puts in a command to have the means for girls and for boys calculated. The computer answers 'cannot compute: undefined variable' or something to that effect. She may become aware that she knows that Simone is a girl and Paul is a boy but *the computer* does not. She may become aware of the meaning of 'variable' in a way that a list of names and of grades might not have provoked. Celia Hoyles, Richard Noss and their colleagues in Mathematical Sciences at the Institute (for a summary, see Noss and Hoyles, 1996) have been investigating the possibility that the need to use procedures that include variables in a variety of examples of mathematical software does in fact provoke this development and have already found some evidence that the use of LOGO can play this role.

In the mathematics world, there are many symbolic objects. I have made my case initially by drawing attention to variables and functions, which are quite easily identified as symbolic objects of thought. But the case I want to make is much broader: that even the simplest operations, like addition and subtraction, are symbolic objects.

When children start school, sometime between five and seven years, depending on the cultural tradition, they already have a conceptual basis for learning about arithmetic operations. Piaget's central thesis was that the basic meanings of arithmetic operations stem from children's schemas of actions – that is, generalizable and structured actions, which can be applied to a variety of objects and which centre on the relations between objects and transformations rather than on the objects *per se*. Children can compare, put things in order, join and separate, make correspondences etc. and connect these action schemas with counting in order to solve problems involving numbers. For example, we can ask them to imagine that a boy had five marbles and then his father gave him two more; how many marbles would the boy have then? A large proportion of five-year olds would solve this problem using the action schema of joining: put up five fingers, put up two more fingers, count them all together. This is an action schema because the child has no interest in the objects, just in the numerical relations. In fact, the problem was solved using fingers but the story was about marbles.

Action schemas provide children with the first meanings for the mathematical signs + and – when these are taught in school. But there is not a simple correspondence between schemas of action and arithmetic operations (as between the fingers and the marbles in the problem above). There are two basic reasons for this lack of correspondence.

First, action schemas can be applied to objects or tokens of objects in a way that they cannot be applied to numerical signs. When children solve a problem using correspondence, they are often unable to say which operation can be used to compute the result. My colleague Constanza Moreno and I recently gave children pictures of objects and asked them to solve a series of problems, one of which was: At a party there are six children and four balloons: How many children won't get balloons? The children had no difficulty in finding out the answer. They counted out six pictures of children, four of balloons, and set them into correspondence. However, a large proportion of the same group of children cannot decide which arithmetic operation might be used to solve this problem. Our results replicate previous observations by Hudson (1983) and also by Marton and Neuman (1990), who did not provide the children with any external support and observed that the children applied the correspondence schema to their fingers. But there is no way in which the elements in the number 'six' can be set in correspondence with those of the number 'four'. Numbers offer a compact representation of the quantity. If the schema of correspondence is used with numerical signs, it cannot be used in the same way.

The second difficulty in connecting schemas of action with arithmetic operations stems from the fact that the same arithmetic operation (for example, addition) is related to different action schemas, which in turn are also connected to other operations. The schema of correspondence, for example, can be used to solve problems that involve the arithmetic operations of addition, subtraction, multiplication and division.[3] Although the schemas of action are used to solve problems and work as a starting point for understanding operations, there is a mismatch between what pupils already know and what they learn in the mathematics classroom. Giordan (1989) stressed that this mismatch is typical of any new learning: 'a new element does not inscribe itself directly on the line of previous knowledge' (p. 251). The signs +, −, x and ÷ are not simply squiggles to record schemas of actions: they are representations of new, socially constructed symbolic objects of thought. When we represent operations with these signs, (paraphrasing Olson's (1996) argument about literacy) the model provides the concepts that make these modes of reasoning conscious.

In summary, mathematics offers learners a variety of symbolic objects of thought, which are themselves frameworks for thinking or models for knowing. In the mathematics classroom, schools have ample opportunity to develop children's minds by engaging them in thinking about these objects.

## *b. Numeracy's tools for thinking*

I want to consider here three types of numeracy tools, which appear to correspond to three levels of artifacts elaborated by Wartofsky (1973). The first type is that of primary artifacts -calculators, rulers, scales, computers and all sorts of software for mathematical purposes, for example. There is no doubt that these tools afford their users considerable advantages; they develop our minds in the literal sense. With a calculator, for example, we can speed up our calculations, be more certain of precision, avoid boredom when a series of computations is necessary. But access to calculators is not 'free', so to speak: we must be able to use the concepts of operations developed in mathematics. Work with unschooled adults (Nunes, 1992), whose reasoning schemas have not been socialized into the particular forms of arithmetic prescribed by school, illustrates this point. Unschooled adults, who are perfectly capable of solving a variety of arithmetic problems in everyday life using their own reasoning schemas, showed marked difficulty when asked to solve missing-addend problems using a calculator. A problem is referred to as a missing addend problem when the situation described involves an increase in a given quantity by an unknown amount yielding a given result; for example: Ann had 84 stamps in her stamp collection; she got some more from her friend and now she has 102. How many stamps did her friend give her? In order to use a calculator to solve a missing addend problem, we have to enter the final amount and subtract the initial amount from it. Although the situation is additive, the arithmetic operation used in the solution is a subtraction. Many unschooled adults solve this problem without the calculator by counting up from the initial amount to the final quantity and keep track of what they have added. For example: 84 plus 10, 94; plus another 10, 20, 104; that means Ann got 18 from her friend. The reasoning is perfectly sound but it does not work with a calculator. To solve the problem with a calculator, we need to enter the subtraction $102 - 84 =$.

This introduces the idea of secondary artifacts: the representations of primary artifacts and the modes of action that support its use. Our observations of children show that even the simplest primary numeracy artifacts cannot be used without a framework for thinking that goes with it. With Paul Light and John Mason, I asked pairs of children (5 and 6 years of age) to measure the length of two lines and decide which one was longer. Each child only had visual access to one line and communicated with the other child by telephone. It soon became clear that not all children could read a ruler. Some of them aligned the end of the ruler with the beginning of the line, ignoring the gap between the end of the ruler and the zero; others placed the number 1 at the end of the line. These children did not seem to realize that each number represents a unit of length counted from the origin, at zero. When asked to put the numbers on an already drawn ruler, the existence of difficulties was confirmed: many children did not use a zero at the origin and a few did not align the numbers with the lines that marked the units of measurement (for further detail, see Nunes and Bryant, 1996). Secondary artifacts are essentially frameworks of thinking. The use of some primary artifacts can be taught and learned through rules or recipes but one then wonders how flexible the use of the artifact will be. If a child is taught the rule 'always place the zero against the beginning of the line you are measuring', what will the child do if the ruler is broken and the first number on it is the 4?. Most likely, the use of the vast majority of numeracy tools can only be learned as frameworks for thinking. Yet, there may be the temptation to teach secondary tools as rules and recipes.

Tertiary artifacts are imaginative ones. They are relatively autonomous representations of the world but can come to colour our world view. Wartofsky applies this conception to works of art but it seems to me just as useful for understanding mathematical models and other theories. Mathematical models are not about the use of any artifact in particular. The comparison between the two types of number introduced earlier on shows that they constitute systems of meaning. Tertiary numeracy tools are very much like the round world or genes: the relationship between encountering tertiary artifacts and development is a probabilistic one. Some people may learn about them as mere facts and others may find in them world views.

## Developing children's minds through literacy and numeracy: A conclusion

The interest in the consequences of literacy has been a multidimensional issue in the last four decades. When UNESCO first declared its intention to eliminate illiteracy, the consequences of literacy were viewed as political, economical, and humanistic. Literacy was expected to 'give people greater control over their local environment and to provide them with more information about the world events affecting their lives' (UNESCO, 1951, in Cole, 1996). The divide between literates and illiterates makes a farce of democratic principles: illiterates simply do not have the same opportunities as literates socially, economically and politically.

Educationalists, anthropologists and psychologists became engaged in the investigation of the consequences of literacy. The expectations seemed initially very high: the shift from utterance to text (Olson, 1976; Goody and Watt, 1963; Luria, 1976) was viewed as the shift from intuition to logical reasoning.

What I propose in this discussion is much more modest but in my view still quite powerful. The evidence regarding the shift from intuition to logic is simply not there. Cole and his colleagues have shown that unschooled people do not lack logical reasoning for lack of literacy (Scribner and Cole 1981) or Western numeracy (Gay and Cole, 1967; Cole, Gay, Glick and Sharp, 1971). But literacy and numeracy equip us with tools which allow us to surpass our natural limits of memory, perception, and processing capacity, amongst other things. They offer us new objects for thought, and these become frameworks for thinking that can be used for further learning. And they also offer us world views, models of objects and situations which we learn to manipulate to further our knowledge. The models are not general rules of logic but systems of meaning within which we can use logic. The connection between encountering these models and the development of our minds is probabilistic: the opportunities may be taken up or they may be missed. The challenge for all of us, teachers and researchers, is to find ways that increase the probability that our students will use rather than miss these opportunities.

## Notes

1. Reprinted with permission from Blackwell. First appeared in Nunes (1995).

2. My translation is free in order to preserve the style.

3. An example of the use of correspondence to solve division problems: I have 12 sweets and there are 3 children; how many sweets will each one get if the distribution is fair? If six year old children have tokens to represent the sweets and the children, they easily set these in correspondence repeatedly and find the result. Similar correspondence procedures are observed in multiplication problems like: there are 4 houses and 2 rabbits inside each house; how many rabbits altogether?

# References

Bateson, G. (1972), *Steps to an ecology of the mind: A revolutionary approach to man's understanding of himself*. New York: Ballantine.

Bindman, M. R. (1997), 'Relashionships between metalinguistic and spelling development across languages: Evidence from English and Hebrew'. Unpublished Ph.D. Thesis, London: Institute of Education, University of London.

Bryant, P. E., and Bradley, L. (1985), *Children's reading problems*. Oxford: Blackwell.

Carraher, T. N. (1987), 'Theoretical and empirical approaches to causality: The case of segmental analysis and literacy'. *European Bulletin of Cognitive Psychology*, 7, 5:456-461.

Cole, M. (1996), *Cultural psychology. A once and future discipline*. Cambridge (Mass): The Belknap Press of Harvard University Press.

Cole, M., Gay, J., Glick, J., and Sharp, D. W. (1971), *The cultural context of learning and thinking*. New York: Basic Books.

da Fontoura, H. A. and Siegel, L. S. (1991), 'Reading, syntactic and working memory skills of bilingual Portuguese-Canadian children'. Unpublished manuscript, University of Toronto, Canada.

Desli, D. And Nunes, T. (1997), 'Are there different types of measuring numbers?' Paper presented at the International Group for the Study of the Psychology of Mathematics Education (PME), July, Lathi (Finland),

Erickson, G. (1985) 'Heat and temperature: an overview of pupils' ideas'. In (Eds.) R. Driver, E. Guesne and A. Tiberghien: *Children's ideas in science*, Milton Keynes: Open University Press.

Ferreiro, E. (1992), *Com todas as letras* (With all the letters), São Paulo: Editora Cortez.

Freudenthal, H. (1983), Didactical phenomenology of mathematical structures. Dordrecht: D. Reidel.

Gay, J. and Cole, M. (1967), *The New Mathematics and an Old Culture*. New York: Holt, Rhinehart and Winston.

Gelman, R., and Gallistel, C.R. (1978), *The child's understanding of number.* Cambridge, Mass: Harvard University Press.

Geva, E., Wade-Woolley, L., and Shany, M. (1993), 'The concurrent development of spelling and decoding in two different orthographies'. *Journal of Reading Behavior,* 25 (4), 383-406.

Giordan, A. (1989), 'Vers un modele didactique d'apprentissage allosterique'. In N. Bednarz and C. Garnier (eds), *Construction des savoirs. Obstacles et conflits,* Ottawa: Editions Agence d'ARC.

Goody, J. (1987), *The interface between the written and the oral.* Cambridge: Cambridge University Press.

Goody, J., and Watt, I. (1963), 'The consequences of literacy'. *Contemporary Studies in Society and History,* 5:304-345.

Gowing, A-M. (1994), 'Leggere o non leggere? That is the question. The integration of Italian and English language skills'. Unpublished MA Dissertation, London: Institute of Education, University of London.

Hamilton, M. (1997), 'Becoming expert: Literacy practices and the development of vernacular knowledge'. Paper presented at the ESRC Seminar Series 'Integrating Research and Practice in Literacy'. December 4-5, Institute of Education, University of London.

Hudson, T. (1983) 'Correspondences and numerical differences between sets'. *Child Development,* 54, 84-90.

Karplus, R., Pulos, S., and Stage, E.K. (1983), 'Proportional reasoning of early adolescents'. In R. Lesh and M. Landau (eds), *Acquisition of mathematics concepts and processes,* London: Academic Press.

Koyré, A. (1898), *A l'aube de la science classique.* Paris: Herman.

Lundberg, I., Frost, J., and Petersen, O. (1988), 'Effects of an extensive program for stimulating phonological awareness in preschool children'. *Reading Research Quarterly,* 23, 263-284.

Luria, A. (1976), *Cognitive development: Its cultural and social foundations.* Cambridge (Mass): Harvard University Press.

Marton, F., and Neuman, D. (1990), 'Constructivism, phenomenology and the origin of arithmetic skills'. In L. Steffe and T. Wood (eds), *Transforming young children's mathematics education: international perspectives,* Hillsdale, NJ: Lawrence Erlbaum Ass.

Noelting, G. (1980) 'The development of proportional reasoning and the ratio concept Part I - Differentiation of stages'. *Educational Studies in Mathematics,* 11, 217-253.

Noss, R. and Hoyles, C. (1996), *Windows on mathematical meanings: Learning cultures and computers.* Dordrecht: Kluwer.

Nunes, T. (1992), 'Ethnomathematics and everyday cognition'. In D. Grouws (ed.), *Handbook for research in mathematics education,* New York: MacMillan.

— (1995), 'Mathematical and scientific thinking'. In V. Lee and P. Das Gupta (eds), *Children's cognitive and language development,* Oxford: Blackwell and The Open University.

Nunes, T. and Bryant, P. E. (1996), *Children doing mathematics.* Oxford: Blackwell.

Nunes, T., Bryant, P. E., and Bindman, M. (1997), 'Morphological spelling strategies'. *Developmental Psychology,* 33(4):637-649.

Nussbaum, J. (1985), 'The earth as a cosmic body'. In R. Driver, R. Guesne, and A. Tiberghien (eds), *Children's ideas in science,* Milton Keynes: The Open University.

Nussbaum, J., and Novack, J. D. (1976), 'An assessment of children's concepts of the earth utilizing structured interviews'. *Science Education,* 60:535-550.

Olson, D. (1976), 'From utterance to text: The bias of language in speech and writing'. *Harvard Educational Review,* 47 (3):257-281.

Olson, D. R. (1996), 'Literate mentalities: Literacy, consciousness of language, and modes of thought'. In D. R. Olson and N. Torrance (eds), *Modes of thought. Explorations in culture and cognition,* Cambridge: Cambridge University Press.

Piaget, J. (1995) *Sociological studies.* London: Routledge (first published as Etudes sociologiques by Librairie Droz, Switzerland, 1965),

Piaget, J., and Inhelder, B. (1975), *The Origin of the Idea of Chance in Children.* London: Routledge and Kegan Paul.

Robinson, R., Goelman, H., and Olson, D. R. (1983), 'Children's understanding of the relation between expressions (what was said) and intentions (what was meant)', *British Journal of Developmental Psychology,* 1:75-86.

Scribner, S. and Cole, M. (1981), *The psychology of literacy*. Cambridge (Mass): Harvard University Press.

Torrance, N., Lee, E. and Olson, D. R. (1992), 'The development of the distinction between paraphrase and exact wording in the recognition of utterances'. Poster presented at the American Educational Research Association (AERA) , April, San Francisco (CA), USA.

UNESCO, 1951. *Learn and Live. A Way out of Ignorance for 1,200,000,000 People.* Paris.

Venezky, R. L. (1995), 'How English is read: Grapheme-phoneme regularity and orthographic structure in word recognition. In I. Taylor and D. R. Olson (eds), *Scripts and Literacy. Reading and Learning to Read Alphabets, Syllabaries and Characters*. Dordrecht: Kluwer.

Vosniadou, S. and Brewer, W. F. (1992), 'Mental models of the earth: A study of conceptual change in childhood'. *Cognitive Psychology*, 24 (4):535-585.

Wagner, D. A., Spratt, J. E. and Ezzaki, A. (1989), 'Does learning to read in a second language always put the child at a disadvantage?' *Applied Psycholinguistics*, 10:31-48.

Wartofsky, M. (1973), *Models*. Dordrecht: D. Reidel.